The Llama
Who Had No
Pajama

BROWNDEER PRESS

HARCOURT BRACE & COMPANY

San Diego   New York   London

The Llama Who Had No Pajama

100 FAVORITE POEMS

WRITTEN BY

MARY ANN HOBERMAN

Illustrated by Betty Fraser

To my children—Denny, Perry, Chuck, and Meg—inspirations all
—M. A. H.

Text copyright © 1998 by Mary Ann Hoberman
Illustrations copyright © 1998 by Betty Fraser

Browndeer Press is a registered trademark of Harcourt Brace & Company.

Library of Congress Cataloging-in-Publication Data
Hoberman, Mary Ann.
The llama who had no pajama; 100 favorite poems / Mary Ann Hoberman; illustrated by Betty Fraser.
p.   cm.
"Browndeer Press."
Summary: An illustrated collection of poems about all sorts of subjects,
including "Wishes," "Ducks," "When I Need a Real Baby," and "Growing."
ISBN 0-15-200111-5
1. Children's poetry, American. [1. American poetry.] I. Fraser, Betty, ill. II. Title.
PS3558.03367L58   1998
811'.54—dc20   95-18491

First edition
A C E F D B

Printed in Singapore

The illustrations in this book were done in Winsor & Newton gouache and watercolor on bristol paper.
The display type was set in Goudy Sans.
The text type was set in Bembo.
Color separations by Bright Arts, Ltd., Singapore
Printed and bound by Tien Wah Press, Singapore
This book was printed on totally chlorine-free Nymolla Matte Art paper.
Production supervision by Stanley Redfern and Ginger Boyer
Designed by Linda Lockowitz

Most of the poems in this collection were first published in the following books: "Applesauce," "Birthdays," "Changing," "Growing," "Hippopotamus," "Indian Pipe," "Meg's Egg," "Timothy Toppin," "Waiters," "Whenever," and "Yellow Butter": *Yellow Butter Purple Jelly Red Jam Black Bread,* text copyright © 1981 by Mary Ann Hoberman, published by The Viking Press; "Ant Song," "B," "Centipede," "Click Beetle," "Cockroach," "Counting-out Rhyme," "Cricket," "Fireflies," "Mayfly," "Mosquito" (O Mrs. Mosquito, quit biting me, please!), "Permutations" ("Combinations"), "Praying Mantis," "Question," "Termite," and "Who Am I? (I)": *Bugs,* text copyright © 1976 by Mary Ann Hoberman, published by The Viking Press; "Balloons" (Balloons to blow), "Cookie Magic" (Cookie cutters), "Ducks" (Ducks are lucky), "Eggs" (Eggs are laid by turkeys), "Good Morning When It's Morning," "Money" (Money's funny), "Nuts to You" (Nuts to you and nuts to me!), "O Is Open," "Windshield Wipers" (Windshield wipers wipe the windshield), and "X?": *Nuts to You and Nuts to Me: An Alphabet of Poems,* text copyright © 1974 by Mary Ann Hoberman, published by Alfred A. Knopf, Inc.; "Advice," "Alligator/Crocodile," "Anteater," "Anthropoids," "Auk Talk," "Bear" (I like to watch the big bear walk), "Camel," "Flamingo," "Foxes," "Gazelle," "Giraffes," "Ocelot," "Panda," "Penguin," "Procyonidae," "Pythons," "Sloth," "Tapir," "Whale," and "Wish" (I'd like to be): *The Raucous Auk,* text copyright © 1973 by Mary Ann Hoberman, published by The Viking Press; "Frog," "How Many?," "Mouse," "Rabbit," "Raccoon," "Riddle" ("Who Am I? [II]")," "Shrew," and "Worm": *A Little Book of Little Beasts,* text copyright © 1973 by Mary Ann Hoberman, published by Simon and Schuster; "Here We Go," "Let's Dress Up," "Oak Leaf Plate," and "When I Need a Real Baby": *Not Enough Beds for the Babies,* text copyright © 1965 by Mary Ann Hoberman, published by Little, Brown and Company; "The Birthday Bus," "Brother," "Butterfish Bay," "A Catch," "Comparisons," ("Comparison"), "Excursion," "Fish," "The Folk Who Live in Backward Town," "Hello and Good-by," "How Far," "I Was Riding to Poughkeepsie," "It's Dark Out," "The King of Umpalazzo," "The Llama Who Had No Pajama," "Look," "Neighbors," "North Pole," "Opposites," "Snow," "A Thought," "Tiger," "Time," "Way Down Deep," "Wishes," and "A Year Later": *Hello and Good-by,* copyright © 1959 by Mary Ann and Norman Hoberman, published by Little, Brown & Company; "Both My Slippers," "Hello, Rain," "Ice-Skating" (In winter when the biting breezes), and "Up and Down the Avenue": *All My Shoes Come in Twos,* copyright © 1957 by Mary Ann Hoberman and Norman Hoberman, published by Little, Brown & Company.

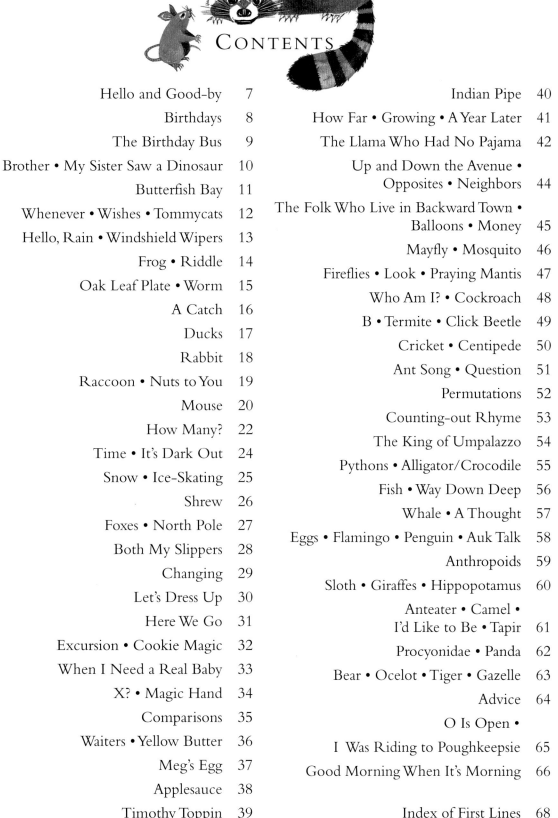

CONTENTS

HELLO AND GOOD-BY

Hello and good-by
Hello and good-by

When I'm in a swing
Swinging low and then high,
Good-by to the ground
Hello to the sky.

Hello to the rain
Good-by to the sun,
Then hello again sun
When the rain is all done.

In blows the winter,
Away the birds fly.
Good-by and hello
Hello and good-by.

BIRTHDAYS

If birthdays happened once a week
Instead of once a year,
Think of all the gifts you'd get
And all the songs you'd hear
And think how quickly you'd grow up;
Wouldn't it feel queer
If birthdays happened once a week
Instead of once a year?

THE BIRTHDAY BUS

My birthday is coming and I will be six;
I'd like a new bike and some peppermint sticks;
But if someone decided to give me a bus,
I'd accept it at once without making a fuss.

I'd tell all of my friends to come quickly inside
And I'd take them all out for a wonderful ride.
If somebody wanted to stop, they'd just buzz
And I'd stop in a minute, wherever I was;
And if somebody had somewhere special to go,
I'd drive there at once and I'd never say no.

The ride would be free; they would each have a seat;
And every half hour I'd hand out a treat.
I'd pull up at a bus stop; I'd put on the brake,
And I'd pass around ice cream and soda and cake.
Then when they were finished, I'd call out, "Hi-ho!
Hold on to your hats, everybody! Let's go!"
(But if anyone asked me to please let them drive,
I'd say driving is dangerous for children of five.)

My birthday is coming and I will be six;
I'd like a new bike and some peppermint sticks;
But if someone decided to give me a bus,
I'd accept it at once without making a fuss.

BROTHER

I had a little brother
And I brought him to my mother
And I said I want another
Little brother for a change.

But she said don't be a bother
So I took him to my father
And I said this little bother
Of a brother's very strange.

But he said one little brother
Is exactly like another
And every little brother
Misbehaves a bit, he said.

So I took the little bother
From my mother and my father
And I put the little bother
Of a brother back to bed.

MY SISTER SAW A DINOSAUR

My sister saw a dinosaur.
At least she said she saw one.
I said that dinosaurs are dead.
She said she saw it in her head.
A dinosaur inside your head?
"Remarkable!" my mother said.

BUTTERFISH BAY

I rowed the boat over to Butterfish Bay
(Butterfish Bay is quite far away).
I took my lunch in a paper sack
And said that I didn't know when I'd be back:
I might get caught in a terrible squall
And then I'd never get back at all,
Or the boat might tip over and I might drown,
Or I might spend the night in Butterfish Town;
All kinds of things happen to ships at sea.
That's all very well, said Mother to me,
As long as you're home at half past three.

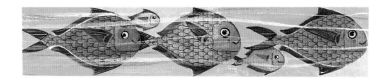

WHENEVER

Whenever I want my room to move,
I give myself a twirl
And busily, dizzily whiz about
In a reeling, wheeling whirl.
Then I spin in a circle as fast as I can
Till my head is weak from churning
Like a tipsy top. . . .
And then I stop.
　　　But my room goes right on turning.

WISHES

I'd like to dress in satin
I'd like to dress in silk
I'd like to have a nanny goat
To give me nanny milk.

I'd like to dress in flannel
I'd like to dress in fur
I'd like to have a pussycat
And listen to her purr.

TOMMYCATS

Big
Black
Tommycats
Are never
Never
Mommycats.

HELLO, RAIN

Hello, rain,
Hello, rain,
Dripping down
The windowpane.
You are wet,
I am dry.
You can't wet me
Though you try,
For when I
Go outside
My umbrella,
Held up high,
And my rubbers
Keep me dry.

WINDSHIELD WIPERS

Windshield wipers wipe the windshield
Wipe the water off the pane
This way   That way
This way   That way
This way   That way
In the rain

FROG

Pollywiggle
Pollywog
Tadpole
Bullfrog
Leaps on
Long legs
Jug-o-rum
Jelly eggs
Sticky tongue
Tricks flies
Spied by
Flicker eyes
Wet skin
Cold blood
Squats in
Mucky mud
Leaps on
Long legs
Jug-o-rum
Jelly eggs
Laid in
Wet bog . . .
Pollywiggle
Pollywog.

RIDDLE

No matter where I travel,
No matter where I roam,
No matter where I find myself,
I always am at home.

Sniffed the snail
In its shell,
"This fact is true
Of me as well."

OAK LEAF PLATE

Oak leaf plate
Acorn cup
Raindrop tea
Drink it up!

Sand for salt
Mud for pie
Twiggy chops
Fine to fry.

Sticks for bread
Stones for meat
Grass for greens
Time to eat!

WORM

Squiggly
Wiggly
Wriggly
Jiggly
Ziggly
Higgly
Piggly
Worm.

Watch it wiggle
Watch it wriggle
See it squiggle
See it squirm!

A Catch

I've caught a fish!
Come look!
I've got him on my hook.
He saw my worm down in the pond,
And fishes all are very fond
Of worms, so up he swam to mine,
And now I've got him on my line.
He's just the proper size to munch.
(I think I'll have him fried for lunch.)

DUCKS

Ducks are lucky,
Don't you think?
When they want to
Take a drink,
All they do is
Duck their bill.
(Doesn't matter
If they spill.)
When they want to
Take a swim,
All they do is
Dive right in;
And they never
Seem to sink.
Ducks are lucky,
Don't you think?

RABBIT

A rabbit
bit
A little bit
An itty-bitty
Little bit of beet.
Then bit
By bit
He bit
Because he liked the taste of it.
But when he bit
A wee bit more,
It was more bitter than before.
"This beet is bitter!"
Rabbit cried.
"I feel a bit unwell inside!"
But when he bit
Another bite, that bit of beet
Seemed quite all right.
Besides
When all is said and done,
Better bitter beet
Than none.

RACCOON

Crash goes the trash can! Clatter and clacket!
What in the world can be making that racket?
I hurry to look by the light of the moon,
And what do I find? Why, a fine fat raccoon!
All through the garden the garbage he's strewn,
And he's eating his supper, that robber raccoon,
Eating so nicely without fork or spoon,
Why, his manners are perfect, that thieving raccoon!
And wasn't he smart to discover that pail?
And wasn't he smart to uncover that pail?
And isn't he lucky he won't go to jail
For stealing his dinner and making a mess
For me to clean up in the morning, I guess,
While he, the old pirate, abundantly fed,
Curls up in a ball fast asleep in his bed?

NUTS TO YOU

Nuts to you and nuts to me!
Walnut, chestnut, hickory,
Butter-, coco-, hazel-, pea-
Nuts to you and nuts to me!

MOUSE

Dear little
Mere little
Merry little
Meadow mouse
    Where do you live? Where do you live?
In a mole's hole
Bird's nest
Hollow of a hickory
    That's where I live. That's where I live.

Dear little
Mere little
Merry little
Meadow mouse
    What do you do? What do you do?
Hunt for food and
Care for my babies
    That's what I do. That's what I do.

Dear little
Mere little
Merry little
Meadow mouse
    What do you eat? What do you eat?

Roots and
Seeds and
Nuts and
Insects
  That's what I eat. That's what I eat.

Dear little
Mere little
Merry little
Meadow mouse
  What do you fear? What do you fear?
Every kind of stranger
Every kind of danger
  That's what I fear. That's what I fear.

Dear little
Mere little
Merry little
Meadow mouse
  What do you love? What do you love?
Running and
Racing and
Chasing round in circles
  That's what I love. That's what I love.

HOW MANY?

A mother skunk all black and white
Leads her babies down the street
    Pitter patter
    Pitter patter
    Pitter patter
    TWENTY feet.

Off they toddle slow and steady
Making tiny twitter cries
    Flitter flutter
    Flitter flutter
    Flitter flutter
    TEN small eyes.

Nose to tail-tip in procession
Single file the family trails
      Flippy floppy
      Flippy floppy
      Flippy floppy
      FIVE long tails.

Up the street a dog comes barking,
Sees the strangers, leaps pell-mell . . .
      Ickle pickle
      Ickle pickle
      Ickle pickle
      ONE BIG SMELL!

TIME

Listen to the clock strike
One
    two
        three,
Up in the tall tower
One
    two
        three.
Hear the hours slowly chime;
Watch the hands descend and climb;
Listen to the sound of time
One
    two
        three.

IT'S DARK OUT

It's dark out
It's dark out
Although the hour's early:
It isn't even five o'clock
And yet it's dark all down the block,
Because the season's winter
And the sun has gone to bed.

SNOW

Snow
Snow
Lots of snow
Everywhere we look and everywhere we go
Snow in the sandbox
Snow on the slide
Snow on the bicycle
Left outside
Snow on the steps
And snow on my feet
Snow on the sidewalk
Snow on the sidewalk
Snow on the sidewalk
Down the street.

ICE-SKATING

In winter when the biting breezes
Blow and all the water freezes,
Then it's time, it's time to go
Skating on the ice.

Choose a day that's bright and clear,
Bundle up from toe to ear;
It's the time, the time of year
For skating on the ice.

I perch upon the snowy rocks
And pull on both my woolen socks;
I lace my skates and tie them fast
And then I'm up and off at last.

I cannot make a figure eight
(I still have trouble going straight),
But just the same I love to skate,
To ice-skate on the ice.

SHREW

The shrew is so busy she makes me quite dizzy
    she always is running she never is still
Her appetite rules her she always is hungry
    she always is hunting to capture her fill
Of spiders and centipedes earthworms and crickets
    garden snakes meadow mice grasshoppers snails
With her long pointed snout she is poking them out
    as she scampers about along tunnels and trails
She never slows down like a sensible animal
    even in winter she dashes around
Chasing and racing through snowdrifts and hollows
    while commonsense creatures are snug underground
But her vigorous life doesn't last the way theirs do
    she lives and she dies within five hundred days
Sniffing and searching through summer and winter
    she wears herself out with her hardworking ways
Until one dark evening on frost-coated stubble
    while out on an errand she stumbles and drops
And her motor runs down
        It gets lower and lower
              Goes slower and slower
                  And finally
                    Stops

FOXES

A litter of little black foxes. And later
A litter of little gray foxes. And later
A litter of little white foxes.
The white ones are lighter than gray. Not a lot.
The gray ones are lighter than black. Just a little.
The litters are lighter in moonlight. They glitter.
They gleam in the moonlight. They glow and they glisten.
Out on the snow see the silver fox sparkle.

NORTH POLE

Have you ever been to the North Pole
Where the frozen world wears a coat of ice
And the sky is white
And the ice is white
And the earth inside
Is closed up tight,
Secret and still and dark as night?

BOTH MY SLIPPERS

Both my slippers
Are bright red.
At night they sit
Beneath my bed,
And in the morning
Off they glide
With my two feet
All snug inside.

CHANGING

I know what *I* feel like;
I'd like to be *you*
And feel what *you* feel like
And do what *you* do.
I'd like to change places
For maybe a week
And look like your look-like
And speak as you speak
And think what you're thinking
And go where you go
And feel what you're feeling
And know what you know.
I wish we could do it;
What fun it would be
If I could try you out
And you could try me.

LET'S DRESS UP

Let's dress up in grown-up clothes:
      Swishing skirts
      That touch our toes;
      Wispy veils
      That hide our nose.
Let's dress up today.

      Feathered bonnet
      Trimmed with lace;
      Rouge and lipstick
      On our face;
      An umbrella
      (Just in case).
Let's dress up today.

Now we're ready.
Let's go walking
Down the street
(Pretend we're talking).
      Walking
      Talking
      Walking
      Talking,
All dressed up today.

HERE WE GO

Here we go
To and fro
Pushing our carriages nice and slow
Up and down
Through the town
Taking a walk with our babies.

Tuck them in
Toe to chin
Shawls fastened tight with a safety pin
Back and forth
South and north
Taking a walk with our babies.

Off they glide
On their ride
Snug in their carriages side by side
Rain or shine
It's so fine
Taking a walk with our babies.

EXCURSION

I put my honey in her pram.
I pushed my honey to the store.
I bought my honey a stick of candy.
Honey said, Now ain't that dandy?
Storeman said, I want some money.
Honey said, Now ain't that funny?
Money for a stick of candy!
Do you have some money handy?
I paid the man a silver dime.
(Had it with me all the time.)
I put my honey in her pram.
I pushed her home
And here I am.

COOKIE MAGIC

Cookie cutters
Cutting cookies
Cutting different
Shapes and sizes
First you make them
Next you bake them
Then you take them
And you cool them
And . . .
That's weird.
They've disappeared!

WHEN I NEED A REAL BABY

When I need a real baby   And can't use my brother,

My dog is my baby   And I am his mother.

I give him a bottle,   I brush out his hair,

I put on his diaper   And booties (two pair);

I tie on his bonnet   And button his smock;

Then into his carriage   And off down the block.

I wave to our neighbors   And stop for a chat,

But leave in a rush   At the sight of a cat.

We have a fine time   As I wheel him about

And he makes a fine baby   Until he jumps out.

X?

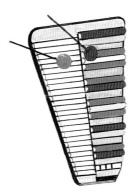

X?
It seldom starts a word,
A well-known word,
A word you've heard.
X-words do not get used a lot.
I knew one once
But I forgot.

MAGIC HAND

I have a magic hand; it looks
Quite normal to one's eyes.
But it can cover anything,
No matter what its size.

My hand can cover houses,
Make a mountain disappear,
Or hide a hippopotamus
If it is not too near.

I have a magic hand; it looks
Quite normal to one's eyes.
But it can cover anything,
No matter what its size.

COMPARISONS

John is the tallest—he's ever so high;
Betty's a little bit taller than I;
I'm not as tall as Betty is tall;
But John is the tallest, the tallest of all.
  Tall, taller, tallest,
  One, two, and three.
  Both John and Betty
  Stretch high over me.
But turn it around and it's better for me
Because I'm the shortest of all the three.
  Short, shorter, shortest,
  Hello and good-by.
  I am the shortest;
  The shortest am I.

Betty's the oldest—six last July;
John isn't six, but he's older than I;
I'm not as old since I'm just over four;
John's a bit older and Betty's much more.
  Old, older, oldest,
  One, two, and three.
  Both John and Betty
  Are years beyond me.
But turn it around and it's better for me
Because I'm the youngest of all the three.
  Young, younger, youngest,
  Hello and good-by.
  I am the youngest;
  The youngest am I.

WAITERS

Dining with his older daughter
Dad forgot to order water.
Daughter quickly called the waiter.
Waiter said he'd bring it later.
So she waited, did the daughter,
Till the waiter brought her water.
When he poured it for her later,
Which one would you call the waiter?

YELLOW BUTTER

Yellow butter purple jelly red jam black bread

Spread it thick
Say it quick

Yellow butter purple jelly red jam black bread

Spread it thicker
Say it quicker

Yellow butter purple jelly red jam black bread

Now repeat it
While you eat it

Yellow butter purple jelly red jam black bread

Don't talk
With your mouth full!

MEG'S EGG

Meg
Likes
A *re*gular egg

Not a poached
Or a fried
But a *re*gular egg

Not a deviled
Or coddled
Or scrambled
Or boiled

But an *eggular*
*Meg*ular
*Re*gular
Egg!

Applesauce

Shall I dig a hole?
Shall I make it deep?
Shall I slope the sides?
Shall I make them steep?
Shall I scoop a path?
Shall I make it wide?
Shall I pile a mountain
      Over on the side?
Shall I point the top?
Shall I push the tip?
Shall I let it slide?
Shall I let it slip?
Shall I let it hide
      The path across the plate?
Shall I curve the path?
Shall I make it straight?
Shall I fill it up?
Shall I smooth it flat?
Shall I draw a dog?
Shall I draw a cat?
Shall I build a house?
Shall I make a street?
Shall I dig a hole?
      Or
Shall I start to eat?

TIMOTHY TOPPIN

Timothy Toppin climbed up a tree—
    He would not come down.
He climbed to the tippety top of the tree—
    He would not come down.
His father and mother were begging him please;
His sister and brother were down on their knees.
"Timothy, Timothy, don't be a tease."
    But he absolutely would not come down.

Timothy Toppin climbed up a tree—
    He would not come down.
He climbed to the tippety top of the tree—
    He would not come down.
"I can touch the sky if I try," said he.
"There isn't a thing that I can't see,
And what's even better, you can't see me
    So why should I ever come down?"

Timothy Toppin stayed seventy years—
    He would not come down.
His mother and father were close to tears—
    He would not come down.
And then when he was seventy-four,
He climbed down the trunk and he walked in the door
And he said, "I don't want to stay up anymore
    And that's why I finally came down."

INDIAN PIPE

Blueberries
Blueberries
Blueberries ripe!
And I just found a clump of Indian pipe
Slender and white at the foot of an oak
Where perhaps long ago a whisper of smoke
Twisted up through the air
And out over this land
As an Indian stood
With his pipe in his hand
Right here in this wood
Right here where I stand.

HOW FAR

How far
How far
How far is today
When tomorrow has come
And it's yesterday?

Far
And far
And far away.

GROWING

The grown-ups say I'm growing tall
And that my clothes are growing small.
Can clothes grow *small*?
I always think
That things grow *big*
Or else they shrink.
But did they shrink
Or did I grow
Or did we both change?
I don't know.

A YEAR LATER

Last summer I couldn't swim at all;
I couldn't even float;
I had to use a rubber tube
Or hang on to a boat;
I had to sit on shore
While everybody swam;
But now it's this summer
And I can!

THE LLAMA WHO HAD NO PAJAMA

The llama who had no pajama
Was troubled and terribly sad
When it became known that he had outgrown
Every pair of pajamas he had;
And he tearfully said to his mama
In a voice that was deep with despair:
O llamaly mama
I need a pajama
Or what in the world will I wear?
Or what in the world,
In the wumberly world,
In the wumberly world will I wear?

The llama who had no pajama
Looked up at the evening sky.
It will soon, he said, be time for bed
And all will be sleeping but I.
And all will be sleeping but I, but I,
And all will be sleeping but I.
For how can a llama go bare to bed,
The little pajamaless llama said,
When the rest of the world,
Of the wumberly world,
Are all wearing pretty pajamas?

The poor little llama's sad mama
Got out her needle and thread.
I'll try to enlarge your pajama,
The llama's sad mama said.
And she stitched and she sewed those pajamas
Till she ran out of plum-colored thread,
But they still were too small for the llama.
O what will we do? Mama said.

For you must have a pair of pajamas
As you cannot go naked to bed;
But where in the world,
In the wumberly world,
Will we find you a pair of pajamas?

They looked in each nook and each cranny;
They looked on each hillock and mound;
But though they saw bathrobes and bonnets,
Pajamas were not to be found.
The clock struck a quarter to seven.
The llama lay down on the ground.
I know I won't sleep, he sniffed sadly,
And his nose made a staying-up sound.

But he did sleep. He dozed off at seven,
And he slept for the rest of the night;
And when he woke up in the morning
To his mama he said with delight:
What a wonderful sleep I've been sleeping all night!
My head feels so clear and my eyes feel so bright.
When we looked for pajamas, how foolish we were.
Why, I sleep so much better in nothing but fur!
It fits me so nicely; it's light as the air;
It's the practical thing for a llama to wear.
And since goats don't wear coats
And doves don't wear gloves
And cocks don't wear socks
And bats don't wear hats,
Well, why in the world,
In the wumberly world,
Should llamas be wearing pajamas?

UP AND DOWN THE AVENUE

Up and down the avenue
I roller-roller-skate
Upon the scratchy sidewalk,
Moving fast and straight.
Up and down the avenue,
Until it's very late
And I am called to supper,
I roller-roller-skate.

OPPOSITES

The opposite of dark is light
The opposite of black is white
The opposite of dull is bright
 And I eat chocolate cake at night.

The opposite of loose is tight
The opposite of peace is fight
The opposite of wrong is right
 A circus is a silly sight.

The opposite of big is small
The opposite of short is tall
The opposite of none is all
 Now watch me bounce my rubber ball.

NEIGHBORS

The Cobbles live in the house next door,
In the house with the prickly pine.
Whenever I see them, they ask, "How are you?"
And I always answer, "I'm fine."
And I always ask them, "Is Jonathan home?"
(Jonathan Cobble is nine.)
I'm Jonathan Cobble's very best friend
And Jonathan Cobble is mine.

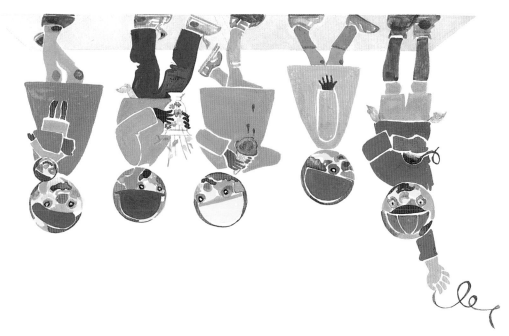

THE FOLK WHO LIVE IN BACKWARD TOWN

The folk who live in Backward Town
Are inside out and upside down.
They wear their hats inside their heads
And go to sleep beneath their beds.
They only eat the apple peeling
And take their walks across the ceiling.

BALLOONS

Balloons to blow
Balloons to burst
The blowing's best
The bursting's worst!

MONEY

Money's funny,
Don't you think?
Nickel's bigger than a dime;
So's a cent;
But when they're spent,
Dime is worth more
Every time.

Money's funny.

MAYFLY

Think how fast a year flies by
A month flies by
A week flies by
Think how fast a day flies by
A Mayfly's life lasts but a day
A single day
To live and die
A single day

How fast it goes
The day
The Mayfly
Both of those.
A Mayfly flies a single day
The daylight dies and darkness grows
A single day
How fast it flies
A Mayfly's life
How fast it goes.

MOSQUITO

O Mrs. Mosquito, quit biting me, please!
I'm happy my blood type with your type agrees.
      I'm glad that my flavor
      Has met with your favor.
      I'm touched by your care;
      Yes, I'm touched, everywhere:
On my arms and my legs, on my elbows and knees,
      Till I cannot tell which
      Is the itchiest itch
      Or which itch in the batch
      Needs the scratchiest scratch.
Your taste for my taste is the reason for these,
So Mrs. Mosquito, quit biting me, please!

FIREFLIES

Fireflies at twilight
In search of one another
Twinkle off and on.

LOOK

Look
Look
Out in the grass
A bumblebee on some sassafras!
Look
Look
Up in the tree
A big black crow and a chickadee!
Look again
On the garden path
A bug in a puddle taking a bath!

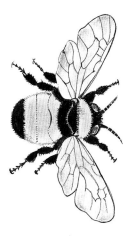

PRAYING MANTIS

That praying mantis over there
Is really not engaged in prayer.
That praying mantis that you see
Is really preying (with an *e*).
It preys upon the garter snake.
It preys upon the bumblebee.
It preys upon the cabbage worm,
The wasp, the fly, the moth, the flea.
(And sometimes, if its need is great,
It even preys upon its mate.)

With prey and preying both so endless,
It tends to end up rather friendless
And seldom is commended much
Except by gardeners and such.

WHO AM I?

A big buzz
In a little fuzz.

COCKROACH

Is there nothing to be said about the cockroach which is kind?
Praise or admiration is impossible to find.
No one seems to care for it or welcome its approaches.
Everyone steers clear of it except for other roaches.
If people treated me that way, I know that I should mind.
Is there nothing to be said about the cockroach which is kind?

Is there nothing to be said about the cockroach which is nice?
It must have done a favor for somebody once or twice.
No one will speak up for it in friendly conversations.
Everyone cold-shoulders it except for its relations.
Whenever it is mentioned, people's faces turn to ice.
Is there nothing to be said about the cockroach which is nice?

Is there nothing to be said about the cockroach which is good?
I can't avoid the feeling that it's quite misunderstood,
But all that I can tell you is it does keep very quiet,
And if you've got some bedbugs, it will add them to its diet.
I'd like to be more positive; I really wish I could.
Is there nothing to be said about the cockroach which is good?

B

A B bred
on B bread
   B comes
A B worker.
A B bred
on B bread
   B comes
A B drone
A B bred
on B bread
cannot B
   A B queen.
   A B queen
      is bred on
      royal jelly
   A   lone.

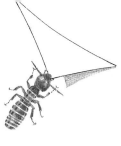

TERMITE

The termite is a decent sort,
Extremely clean, from all report,
Fights only as a last resort.
If only . . .

A skillful worker, so they state,
Builds tunnels at a rapid rate,
Is willing to cooperate.
If only it . . .

Is hard of hearing, so they find,
And cannot see. Poor thing is blind,
Yet lives in friendship with its kind.
If only it would . . .

Is loyal to its queens and kings,
Does not give bites or pricks or stings,
Does not eat other living things.
*If only it would stop eating tables and
chairs and books and houses and baseball
bats and orange trees, then maybe people
could begin to appreciate its good qualities.*

CLICK BEETLE

Click beetle
Clack beetle
Snapjack black beetle
Glint glitter glare beetle
Pin it in your hair beetle
Tack it to your shawl beetle
Wear it at the ball beetle
Shine shimmer spark beetle
Glisten in the dark beetle
Listen to it crack beetle
Click beetle
Clack beetle

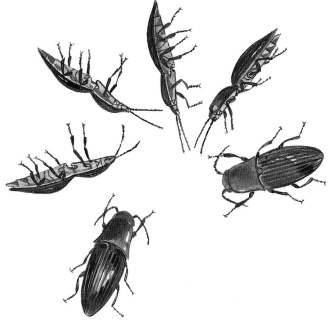

CRICKET

A cricket's ear is in its leg.
A cricket's chirp is in its wing.
A cricket's wing can sing a song.
A cricket's leg can hear it sing.

Imagine if your leg could hear.
Imagine if your ear could walk.
Imagine if your mouth could swing.
Imagine if your arm could talk.

Would everything feel upside down
And inside out and wrong side through?
Imagine how the world would seem
If you became a cricket, too.

CENTIPEDE

A dollar is a hundred cents.
A century's a hundred years.
A centigrade thermometer?
    A hundred degrees
    From boil to freeze.

> *On all these facts*
> *We are agreed;*
> *But what about*
> *A centipede?*

A pedal's pedaled by a foot.
A pedestal's a column's foot.
And what is a pedestrian?
    Someone whose feet
    Walk down the street.

> *That's very fine.*
> *That's fine indeed.*
> *Now what about*
> *A centipede?*

ANT SONG

The queen of ants she lays the eggs.
The males mate with the queen.
The workers find the food to eat
And keep the nest all clean.
The soldiers fight the enemy.
The nurses feed the young.
Ant on
Ant on
Ant on
Ant on
Ant now my song is sung.

QUESTION

Did you ever ever ever think
That every ant you've ever seen
Must be a princess or a prince
Because its mother is a queen?

"Remember me!"
Buzzed the bee.
"I am also
Royalty."

PERMUTATIONS

A flea flew by a bee. The bee
To flee the flea flew by a fly.
The fly flew high to flee the bee
Who flew to flee the flea who flew
To flee the fly who now flew by.

The bee flew by the fly. The fly
To flee the bee flew by the flea.
The flea flew high to flee the fly
Who flew to flee the bee who flew
To flee the flea who now flew by.

The fly flew by the flea. The flea
To flee the fly flew by the bee.
The bee flew high to flee the flea
Who flew to flee the fly who flew
To flee the bee who now flew by.

The flea flew by the fly. The fly
To flee the flea flew by the bee.
The bee flew high to flee the fly
Who flew to flee the flea who flew
To flee the bee who now flew by.

The fly flew by the bee. The bee
To flee the fly flew by the flea.
The flea flew high to flee the bee
Who flew to flee the fly who flew
To flee the flea who now flew by.

The bee flew by the flea. The flea
To flee the bee flew by the fly.
The fly flew high to flee the flea
Who flew to flee the bee who flew
To flee the fly who now flew by.

Counting-out Rhyme

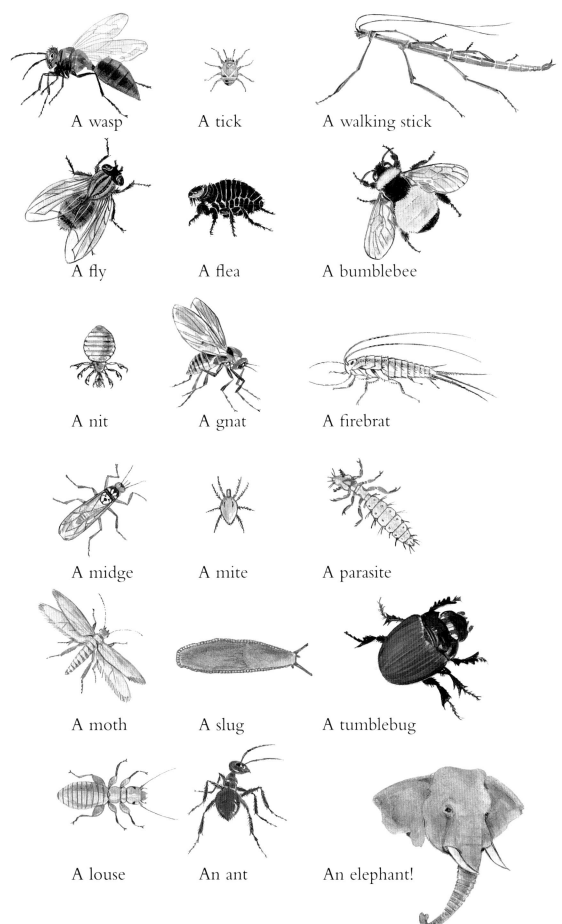

A wasp A tick A walking stick

A fly A flea A bumblebee

A nit A gnat A firebrat

A midge A mite A parasite

A moth A slug A tumblebug

A louse An ant An elephant!

THE KING OF UMPALAZZO

O the King of Umpalazzo
Is very big and fat.
He eats raw steak and chocolate cake
And grouse and mouse and rat,
And veal and eel and Hudson seal
And cracker meal and lemon peel
And dogs that bark and pigs that squeal.
What *do* you think of that?

O the King of Umpalazzo
Is very, very old.
His beard is long and yellow,
His feet are always cold.
His face is full of wrinkles,
His eyesight is quite dim.
He's a silly old billy
Who's always too chilly.
What *do* you think of him?

O the King of Umpalazzo
Is very, very nice.
He says "I thank you" once a day
And he says "You're welcome" twice.
He nods his head and tips his hat
And shakes your hand and walks his cat.
He never tells you not to speak
And he gives out ice cream every week.
He's a funny old honey,
As soft as a bunny.
What *do* you think
  What *do* you think
    What *do* you think of that?

PYTHONS

The thick black pythons
Are braided tight together.
How do they untwine?

ALLIGATOR/CROCODILE

The crocodile
Has a crooked smile.
The alligator's smile is straighter.

Or maybe it's the other way.
(With crocodiles it's hard to say.)

Perhaps the opposite is true.
(It's hard with alligators, too.)

But if I write what I just said,
The first way might be right instead.

And then again the second might
As easily be wrong as right.

Or right as wrong. Likewise the first.
In that case should they be reversed?

Or left alone? Or should I switch?
I can't remember which is which!

The crocodile
Has a crooked smile?
The alligator's smile is straighter?

FISH

Look at them flit
Lickety-split
Wiggling
Swiggling
Swerving
Curving
Hurrying
Scurrying
Chasing
Racing
Whizzing
Whisking
Flying
Frisking
Tearing around
With a leap and a bound
But none of them making the tiniest
                                    tiniest
                                        tiniest
                                            tiniest
                                                sound.

WAY DOWN DEEP

Underneath the water
Way down deep
In sand and stones and seaweed
Starfish creep
Snails inch slowly
Oysters sleep
Underneath the water
Way down deep.

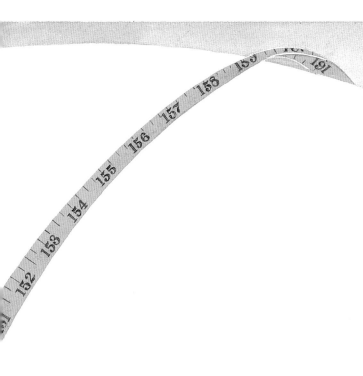

WHALE

A whale is stout about the middle,
He is stout about the ends,
& so is all his family
& so are all his friends.

He's pleased that he's enormous,
He's happy he weighs tons,
& so are all his daughters
& so are all his sons.

He eats when he is hungry
Each kind of food he wants,
& so do all his uncles
& so do all his aunts.

He doesn't mind his blubber,
He doesn't mind his creases,
& neither do his nephews
& neither do his nieces.

You may find him chubby,
You may find him fat,
But he would disagree with you:
He likes himself like that.

A THOUGHT

Think of a whale.
Then
Think of a snail.
Then
Think of a snail on the tail of a whale.
Then
Think of the tail of the whale with no snail.

A whale is so big
And a snail is so small
That there's hardly a difference at all
    between
The snail on the tail
And the tail
With no snail.

EGGS

Eggs are laid by turkeys
Eggs are laid by hens
Eggs are laid by robins
Eggs are laid by wrens
Eggs are laid by eagles
Eggs are laid by quail,
Pigeons, parrots, peregrines—
And that's how every bird begins.

FLAMINGO

Sea risen sunbird
O flaming flamingo, spread
Wide your red feathers.

PENGUIN

O Penguin, do you ever try
To flap your flipper wings and fly?
How do you feel, a bird by birth
And yet for life tied down to earth?
A feathered creature, born with wings
Yet never wing-borne. All your kings
And emperors must wonder why
Their realm is sea instead of sky.

AUK TALK

The raucous auk must squawk to talk.
The squawk auks squawk to talk goes

ANTHROPOIDS

The next time you go to the zoo
The zoo
Slow down for a minute or two
Or two
    And consider the apes,
    All their sizes and shapes.
For they all are related to you
To you.

Yes, they all are related to you
To you
And they all are related to me
To me
    To our fathers and mothers,
    Our sisters and brothers,
And all of the people we see
We see.

The chimpanzees, gorillas, and all
And all
The orangutans climbing the wall
The wall
    These remarkable creatures
    Share most of our features,
And the difference between us is small
Quite small.

So the next time you go to the zoo
The zoo
Slow down for a minute or two
Or two
    And consider the apes,
    All their sizes and shapes,
For they all are related to you
To you.

SLOTH

A tree's a trapeze for a sloth.
He clings with his claws to its growth.
    Both the sloth and his wife
    Lead an upside-down life.
To lead such a life I'd be loath.

GIRAFFES

I like them.
Ask me why.
    Because they hold their heads so high.
    Because their necks stretch to the sky.
    Because they're quiet, calm, and shy.
    Because they run so fast they fly.
    Because their eyes are velvet brown.
    Because their coats are spotted tan.
    Because they eat the tops of trees.
    Because their legs have knobby knees.
    Because
    Because
    Because. That's why
I like giraffes.

HIPPOPOTAMUS

How far from human beauty
Is the hairless hippopotamus
With such a square enormous head
And such a heavy botamus.

ANTEATER

The anteater
The anteater
It hasn't any teeth
   Neither in the jaw above
   Nor in the jaw beneath.

The anteater
The anteater
It hardly has a jaw.
   Without a jaw
   Without some teeth
   It cannot chew or gnaw.

   Its tongue is long and sticky.
   Its snout is long and thin.
   Its mouth is very little
   So little food fits in.

   With such an apparatus
   It can't eat meat or plants.
   No plants? No meat?
   What *can* it eat?
The anteater
Eats

CAMEL

The camel has a heavy bump
      upon his back.
     It's called a hump.
Although it weighs him down, he moves
      with perfect grace
      upon his hooves.

I'D LIKE TO BE

I'd like to be
A kangaroo
And have a pocket
Made of me.

TAPIR

The tapir has a tubby torse.
He is not very big.
Although related to the horse,
He looks more like a pig.

If I were in the tapir's shoes
(Although I'm not of course),
Relation to the pig I'd choose,
Resemblance to the horse.

PROCYONIDAE

If you give a little whistle,
You might meet a cacomistle,
A coati or olingo
Or a raccoon with a ring-o;
I can name them by the dozens
And all of them are cousins
  And they're all related to the giant panda!

The kinkajou's another
That is practically a brother
To coatis and olingos
And to raccoons with their ring-os;
And every single one of them
Is different, that's the fun of them,
  Yet every one's related to the panda!

Now they all have different faces
And they live in different places
And they all have different sizes,
Different noses, different eyeses;
But the family name for all of them
Is just the same for all of them
  And each one is related to the panda!

PANDA

A panda
Planned a visit
But they told him not to come.
He was going to Uganda
(Where of course he isn't from).

Everybody knows the panda
Comes from China not Uganda
And a
Panda
In Uganda
Would cause panda-monium.

BEAR

I like to watch the big bear walk
When I go to the zoo;
Sometimes
Four feet
Seem
Two
Too
Much
And up he goes on two.

Then after he has strolled about
And roared an awful roar,
Sometimes
Two feet
Seem
Two
Too
Few
And down he goes on four.

OCELOT

The ocelot's a clever cat.
She knowsalot of this and that.
She growsalot of spotted fur
Which looks extremely well on her.

In places where it snowsalot
She seldom ever goesalot.
She much prefers it where it's hot.
That's all about the ocelot.

TIGER

I'm a tiger
Striped with fur
Don't come near
Or I might *grrr*
Don't come near
Or I might growl
Don't come near
Or I might
BITE!

GAZELLE

O gaze on the graceful gazelle as it grazes
It grazes on green growing leaves and on grasses
On grasses it grazes, go gaze as it passes
It passes so gracefully, gently, O gaze!

ADVICE

If you're sleepy in the jungle
And you wish to find a pillow,
Take a friendly word of warning:
DO NOT USE AN ARMADILLO!

Though an armadillo often
May roll up just like a pillow,
Do not go by his appearance
But go by with ample clearance.

For an armadillo's armor
Is not suited for a pillow,
And an armadillo's temper
Only suits an armadillo.

If you use him for a pillow,
Then beware of what will follow:
He may slip out while you're sleeping
And an arm or two he'll swallow.

> (And any beast that leaves you armless
> Can't be classified as harmless!)

Nor will he beg your pardon
For his thoughtless peccadillo;
So the next time you go walking in the jungle
TAKE A PILLOW!

O Is Open

O is open
O is round
O's a circle
O's a sound
O's a wheel
O's a hoop
O's an orbit
O's a loop
O's a ring
Made of gold
O's a moon
Halfway old.

I Was Riding to Poughkeepsie

I was riding to Poughkeepsie
When I met a green-eyed gypsy,
A green-eyed Spanish gypsy
In a gold and scarlet gown.

And she told me she was roaming
From Poughkeepsie to Wyoming,
Through the West to wild Wyoming
Where the icy winds blow down.

Ride beside me through the mountains,
By the bubble-blowing fountains,
Said the green-eyed Spanish gypsy
In her gold and scarlet gown.

But I left the green-eyed gypsy
And continued to Poughkeepsie,
Up the highway to Poughkeepsie,
Up to plain Poughkeepsie town.

Good Morning When It's Morning

Good morning when it's morning
Good night when it is night
Good evening when it's dark out
Good day when it is light
Good morning to the sunshine
Good evening to the sky
And when it's time to go away
Good-by
Good-by
Good-by.

INDEX OF FIRST LINES